Rumors of Fallible Gods

also by Peter Ludwin

A Guest In All Your Houses

Rumors of Fallible Gods

Peter Ludwin

PRESA PRESS
ROCKFORD, MI

ACKNOWLEDGMENTS

The poems in this collection first appeared in the following magazines: *Aries, The Bitter Oleander, California Quarterly, The Comstock Review, The Fourth River, Hawai'i Pacific Review, Homestead Review, The Hurricane Review, Kyoto Journal, Lake Effect, Lullwater Review, The Midwest Quarterly, Nimrod, Oyez Review, The Pacific Review, Poem, Presa, Quercus Review, The Raven Chronicles, Red Wheelbarrow, River Oak Review, RiverSedge, Salamander, Tiger's Eye, Tribeca Poetry Review, The Warwick Review, Whiskey Island Magazine, White Heron,* and the *Wisconsin Review.*

First Edition

Printed in the United States of America

ISBN: 978-0-9831251-8-1

Library of Congress Control Number: 2012906406

Cataloging Information: 1. Ludwin, Peter, 1942 ;
2. Contemporary American Poetry

PRESA PRESS
PO Box 792   Rockford, Michigan 49341
presapress@aol.com   www.presapress.com

Rumors of Fallible Gods

for Lois, Diana and Lisa: the three magicians

Contents

Tracking The Minotaur

Light In San Miguel

The Women at Satevó

In the painting, Tarahumaras
huddle outside a church. Overseers
passed down through generations
nest unseen in their headscarves.

They do not smile, these women.
Rather, their faces are furrows of earth
gashed open by pickaxe and plow.
A great weight inclines them

like snow on a cedar branch.
Their tongues harbor smoke
no priest can detect.
If it diffuses behind the eyes,

does fire truly consume the forest?
To endure is an art masked in stone.
Like a trickle from an underground spring,
what they show conceals the marrow:

a New World
still struggling to be born.
It will appear as a rumpled shawl,
the incurable ache of lavender.

Metamorphosis

You have become, let us say, a butterfly,
one of those large monochromatic insects
you saw flitting above the Cuyabeno River.
Orange or solid blue, the colors brilliant

in dappled light. You have always sought
the first waterfall within memory, hungered
not so much to enter the mist as to generate it,
genie-like, from your own internal spark.

To inhabit the transparent pearl, the drop
in perpetual motion that spells a history,
tumbles with no beginning, no end
and never, ever lands.

Resilient

Flagstones glisten from a rare winter rain.
Two nights ago the plaza thronged with people
to welcome the new year. I wandered
among children who bounced
missile-shaped balloons off the pavement,
followed the brilliant flight of sparklers
men twirled outside the cathedral.
My pleasure then was tequila-flavored ice cream,
an archangel rafting a river of smoke,
Andean songs on churango and bamboo flute,
Mexico's restive spirit, "La Llorona."
Who could *not* listen
as women with lacquered fingernails spoke
fables that blossomed like a collage?
Now only a handful are left from the storm.
A pair of lovers, stragglers who can't go home.
Mariachis, not always in tune, still play.
Even trumpets are saddened by water.

Batopilas Canyon to Huimayvo

This is how it begins:
for an hour
we bounce along a dirt road
in Manuel's truck,
beat up couches all that keep us
from bones too bruised to cry.

At the trailhead
we switchback down to the river
and the slender suspension bridge,
graceful as a woman's calf,
that carries us across.

From here on, we step
where mad angels bloom.

When the trail disappears
into near vertical rock,
few slabs to grip, a drop-off below,
all my lives shimmer like heat waves
broiled on the desert's grill.

I stretch out my hand,
and they recede just beyond it.
Tarahumaras can cover this ground
barefoot without looking or slowing down.

How does a person grow wings?

Beyond that short, tough stretch
we boulder hop
a smaller stream from the northwest,
the stones bigger than my car.
The pools they guard
anchor my sky blue breath.

Sounding the alarm, birds
high up the canyon walls lift off.

Rumors of fallible gods.

Huimayvo

What world is this?
One where spiders dream.
Drunk on corn beer,
they scuttle homeward
rubbing the moon on their bellies.

I listen to a sick woman moan
while another grinds *maíz pozolero* into meal.
Baskets and violins
rest on the ground for sale
to the rare gringo who makes it this far:

a backcountry pueblo whose Tarahumara
live in bare earth shelters
among orange trees and goats,
one side open to air,
the other buttressed by rock.

Except for coins that sometimes change hands,
the outside barely ripples here.
The river always flows, and the cliffs
upstream, flushed a deepening crimson,
form the gateway to snake and drum.

How long? Always the question
for the sticky web
suspended in the corner
before the flashlight intrudes
and the dust broom sweeps it away.

In Chihuahua, in San Miguel,
the drowned voice goes begging.
Where do they spend the night,
those Indian women
huddled on narrow flagstone sidewalks,

arms extended, eyes black ponds
that see nothing, not even memory?

Celia

Married with three kids, she's driven
cab in Mexicali for years. *Esto no sirve,*
she tells me. This isn't working.
But what else can she do while she waits
for papers that may never come? The key
to the other side— *al otro lado*-- the land
where money drifts down from the sky.
Like so many Mexicans, she wants to know:
Single? Married? A girlfriend?
When I tell her I'm single and have no kids
it comes as a surprise, even a shock.
Why, she wonders as she describes
the joys of sex. I've had this conversation
before, smiled and shrugged my shoulders.
How can I explain in my basic Spanish—
good enough to get around, hopeless
for such discussion—that sometimes
the *sirocco* comes up, the hot desert wind
that drives men with hollow eyes
raving into the street,
eyes even the moon declines to enter?
Or how doubt can bore like a beetle into choice,
leave a perforated husk that rasps
like brittle stalks of corn? How when that happens
one becomes like the captain of a three-masted ship
who ponders where to drop anchor—
this bay or that cove—and in that moment
of indecision discovers the tide has gone out,
a reef gashed his timbers, water is pouring into the hold...

Demarcation

Last night flames gutted a clothing store in the market.
Today I must visit the dentist. I see portents everywhere.
In the fire, the man who eviscerates a stingray,
the woman chopping a fish into sections
by pounding her machete with a club,
the greedy pelicans who scrimmage
for entrails too large to swallow in one gulp.
All point toward needles and drills,
the stench of slow dismemberment.

This morning, after dropping off my dirty clothes
at the *lavandería*, I walk past tubs of shrimp.
Mazatlán stinks of the sea, of dead creatures
hauled from its depths. But lovers entwined
on the *malecón* germinate seed pods
that ripen like mangoes.

If not for my mouth I could take the boat
to Stone Island. Martín rents horses there.
We would ride along the surf's sibilant edge,
our only truth the motion of horse and wind.
His stained, worn teeth a map of Mexico,
a record of smoke and dung.

Tonight after the novocaine wears off
I will look for Sergio at a blues bar.
Revived by his drums, a band in the *plazuela*
playing "Sweet Home Alabama"
as a girl melting under her boyfriend's touch
whispers *Ah gracias! Gracias por todo!*

Letter to Pablo Neruda from Playa Olas Altas, Mazatlán

Today I think of you, Pablo, at Isla Negra.
Of voluptuous stones beveled by water
into hips you grasped with ache, with hunger
like the moon hugging turtles newly hatched.
How the ocean itself redeemed you, scuttled
the leg iron others tried to fashion

with hammer and tongs, the cooling hiss a brand.
And what of motion, that second actor onstage?
Relentless groover scalloping the earth,
a chisel peeling fragrant curls of wood.
Who better than you to celebrate this marriage?
Body as water seeking, *needing* a tidal pulse.

Captive to this land of drug lords, of women
more stunning than the sea, I watch surfers duck
under rollers as they paddle—their tumbles into spume,
boards upended—when the pipeline takes them out.
This, Pablo, is the sound I wake to each morning.
The music I drink like I inhale your carnal lines,

augur from both the hummingbird, the fleshy
blue guitar. At dusk an emblazoned sky
invokes a language only the wounded know.
The kind that appears one day on palace walls.
What's sinful is not to live. I walk out into streets
filled with seers, prophets, poets of milky jade.

Pelicans

I never tire of their wheel and glide,
how they peel off, wings at the last instant
folded back, and detonate the sea.
Dive bombers of Playa Norte, of Playa Olas Altas,
they sew the languid dreams of baitfish

with a terror Polish peasants knew, those
streams of refugees with their horse-drawn carts
blitzed by the German advance.
Each morning at Playa Norte pelicans scavenge
 an easy bounty. Poised a step out of range,

they lunge to gulp the guts tossed their way
by fishermen cleaning their catch.
But it's the sudden explosion, the bolt
of spray shocked from the incoming tide,
that arrests the eye. Reveals as few

things can that line
where beauty and violence blur,
one not just hinting with collaboration,
the savage glint forged by sun and wave,
but the face—indisputable—of the other.

Canonized

The spiritual lives of drug traffickers are very complicated.
—Froylan Enciso

They hanged you in 1909, a thief
the common people said stole
from the rich and gave to the poor.
Or so the story goes. Some, afraid
of your power, insist you are only a myth.
But look at you now, Jesús Malverde!
At your shrine in Culiacán snapshots
of marijuana plants and AK-47s, known here
as "goat horns," crowd the walls. Women
brush flowers dipped in water across your face.
You have your own beer.
Hotels feature you in their guides.
Eligio González built the shrine to thank you
for healing him after being knifed and shot by bandits.
Moisés García claims you helped him
kick his gambling addiction.

And you have company.

In Tijuana migrants pray for safe crossing
to Juan Soldado, an executed rapist.
Young men flex biceps tattooed with Santa Muerte,
a long-robed skeleton with a scythe.
Others flock to Jude Thaddeus, who Catholics
say aids those with desperate causes.
But who could compete with a patron saint
of drug traffickers named Jesus?
And not just Jesus, but Jesus Evil Green?

So here's to you, Malverde. You're a rock star,
more present in death than you ever were in life.
If some think it a little bizarre,
what does it matter, *hombre*?
This is Mexico.
And who holds a monopoly on the peculiar?
People have prayed forever

to stone and wooden idols, golden calves,
sun and moon, Ba-al, Moloch, Satan,
magical snakes, Earth mothers, virgin mothers,
ascetics, plants that get them high,
witches, demons,
gods of semen and the dance.

And to an obscure desert carpenter.

Transition

When I cross the border
the vulture is waiting.
He meets me there,
black form perched on a saguaro,
eye ravaging the dead dog
whose entrails redden the dust.

Instantly my beard
sprouts like alfalfa
and my checkbook
crumbles to ash.

The vulture becomes my companion,
my guide along the rutted
road to the interior,
the mirror I search
for a sign of my blue-flowered heart.
Dressed like *penitentes* with hidden revolvers,
we stop in a small Sonoran town
that's forgotten its own name.
I follow the vulture
down an alley littered with bones
that murmur *triste, triste,*
inhaling the rumor that the Lone Ranger
has filed off the rowels of his spurs.

Near the last shanty
we find him in bed with a Mexican woman
who braids skulls of sugar candy into his hair.
The fabled mask hangs from a post
anchored in the dirt floor,
its frayed edges alive with wagon trains
where roaches gnaw crumbs

of lost innocence.
He's fat and has six kids
and sometimes, he says,
when lizards crawl across a moon
that hovers just *so*
over brooding thickets of mesquite,
he makes leather wallets
for tourists heading south.
He hasn't seen Tonto
since his faithful companion
melted down the last silver bullets
into convertible IOUs
and left for San Francisco
to learn electric guitar.

He hopes he never
sees Orange County again.

Unlocking the Door

In Chihuahua the vulture again holds me hostage.
Belting out a *narcocorrido*,
he floors the pedal,
hellbent for women who moan.
Music blares from a cheap radio
that threatens to fly apart with the bus.
Near Parral *federales* toting machine guns
stamped with the Madonna
set up roadblocks to stop him.
But the vulture swigs his tequila
and bribes them with showers
of yellow cactus blossoms.
He honks and beats out a rhythm
on the steering wheel,
toasting the Holy Mother
as he slides toward a bottomless ravine.
When I turn around a virgin
seduces the emperor of Japan.
He abdicates,
citing irreconcilable differences,
and steps off the bus
to find the lost pueblo
whose villagers ride unicorns at dawn.

The vulture
skids to a stop in the plaza,
rousting chickens and dust.
Under bursting fiesta lights,
the jangle of brass and guitars,
Disney, McDonald's—
all the numbing afflictions—
begin to fall away
like patterns of childhood illness,

the mottled skin of a sand toad.
Memory, old and visceral as the cells,
emerges unaffected by age.
It comes out wet
and trembling and shining,
dragging its afterbirth,
a slick fawn

that staggers
to a tentative stance.
Drinks from the wild
river in its throat.

Friday Night in San Luis Potosí

The hot boys are cool tonight,
    so cool and so hot
        you give them instant love,

these not quite punks
    taking over the gazebo
        with their boom box

banging out a trip-hammer beat,
    their bodies a taut, hard-wired
        arrogance only the young can know.

Like cocks taking their rivals'
    measure, each dancer
        tries to out-flaunt his friends

as the hens cluck coyly behind.
    Poor bastards. They probably think
        they can do this forever,

that their coiled, steel spring flesh
    will not betray them,
        will never sell them out.

And who am I to say otherwise?
    Jerking and spinning, twisting their limbs
        into figures that make my own

muscles beg for deliverance,
    they explode over the wooden boards.
        First one, then another, the best of them

doing a one-armed handstand while his legs
        scissor kick the air,
                then bouncing across the floor

on that hand, still flailing,
        and finally, as if all to this point
                were mere prelude

to the main contorted act,
        on his forearm,
                elbow cushioned by a pad.

When they are old
        and crippled by arthritis
                I wonder if their sons will believe

the outlandish tales they tell.
        How they spat in gravity's face,
                corralled the beat and *flew*.

Or if they will wink knowingly
        as their friends
                snicker under their breath

at the audacity
        of these grizzled neighbors
                whose voices rasp

like guitar strings tuned too low.
        These *viejos* who lean back and smile.
                Lick lime and salt from their wrists.

Two Doors in Morelia

Maybe ten feet high,
    the strips of studded metal
        beaten with a hammer

into iron flame forked blue.
    They were meant to dazzle,
        these doors, to stop the breath

like Mary Magdalene
    peeling her undergarment
        over plum-rich hips

while a lowly butcher gasped
    and bit his tongue.
        Whoever labored here

craved the core of things,
    a dream of honeyed flesh
        chipped and lathed and sanded down

from packed fiber
    run true to the grain,
        then varnished by a craftsman's hand.

Infused the very pulp
    with a force he could not name
        but only bow to in surrender.

That which sputtered, smoked,
    then sparked a feathery duff,
        scorched the whole design to shape it,

to yield its reluctant form.
    Nothing fancy, no filigreed script
       etched in the wood

like snakes. Rather,
    the unadorned as mirror
       to the slim, naked nail,

to an old man
    lodged within the carver
       himself.   Curled like a fist,

he struggles to rise,
    to whisper in a cupped ear.
       His the voice of shattered worlds.

Breakfast in Baja
for Russell Salamon

Restaurant Jalisco, the sign read,
    a two-room adobe hovel
        sticking up like a wart

from the desert floor. *Noooo,*
    you said, *it's too funky,*
        we 'll get something nobody's got a cure for,

but we went in anyway
    to the little patio
        with its lone table covered with sand,

which the old man's wife
    swept away with her hand
        before she took our order.

You didn't want anything
    but she misunderstood
        and brought out two plates

of eggs and beans and tortillas,
    which we had to eat or insult them
        and slink away like whipped dogs,

and you grudgingly conceded how good it was
    while she kept bringing more plates
        of tortillas without us saying a word,

and avocados,
    and chickens ran by from the garden
        and three kids kept trying

to get the radio to work
    by beating on it with a hammer
        and the old man

went about his chores
    hauling buckets of water back and forth,
        the two meals coming to about $1.75.

Do you remember, my friend, how that
    breakfast lasted all the way to San Felipe,
        where the pelicans flocked to greet us?

Tlacolula Market

Walk with me past stalls
where images of Ché,

another bearded rebel,
compete side by side with Christ.

Scan rows of Zapotec women
hunkered behind enormous onions.

When fireflies light their breasts,
an ocean sweeps their skirts.

It will carry you past mounds
of fried grasshoppers,

past voices pledged to burn,
to liquefy glass with no fuel.

This morning, like quetzals
bursting from cloud forest,

we arrive to bear witness.
Don't these dyed geometries

hung from rug vendors' racks
make you want to wrestle a woman

in plowed earth? Color is a god
we meet on our own terms.

Not with bowed head but erect,
eyes wide open. A weave begins

with one thread looped over
and under. Each plume,

each golden strand a covenant
with the world as cochineal

splits the hungry mirror, sows
a web of corn dream and song.

Existential

Every winter when I return to San Miguel
I find you in the same spot
under the little stone bridge: Carmela,
the *gordita* woman, a *mestiza* crone

one step removed from the shriveled Indian
begging in a doorway like a starving bird.
For thirty years you've made *empanadas*
filled with cheese and hot chilies
on your *comal,* hand dipped in a bucket

of tainted water I ignore. What are you
if not the chime of the tolling bell?
Mexico's true constant, a blue feather
waltzing with dust? Revolutions, coups,

cartels—they come and they go, rank winds
that sear the eyebrows and ravish unsuspecting nuns.
You remain, the lines and folds of your skin
the paths of ruined armies, of obsidian blades
and Spanish bayonets kicked up by a plowing mule.

Once, coming down from the Andes,
an old man asked me *What is your faith?*
I knew what he wanted: that identity card like
American Express. Inconceivable

I would ever leave home without it.
A casualty, that faith, like so many others
in the course of learning to stand naked.
More reliable those simple things that anchor
the common rhythm: a rooster, a bougainvillea.

And you, *gordita* woman?
I believe in you as others believe
in Exxon or the *New York Times,*
the way I used to believe in the Lone Ranger,

a masked redeemer unscarred by doubt,
a range rider whose shirts never creased.
What I see is what I get. Digging for change,
you feed me in places neither of us
has drawn on our worn, tattered maps.

Regeneration

In the Blue House of Frida Kahlo
pain showers beauty into this
bright room, that wild garden.

Cries of street vendors swirl upward,
smoky wisps among the balconies
where lost lovers drift like seaweed.

Each day since my arrival
I tumble from an embryonic moon.
Gather *la cosecha*, the harvest night provides.

Now fire begins to relearn its language.
The art of burning in water.
Cast against the boundary wall,

its unruly tongue fleshes out a figure
from a torn cocoon:
the *mariposa* testing its wings.

For an Indian Girl Asleep in a Tiny Hammock, San Miguel Market

Daughter of earth,
believe this rain
that does not fall,
the hummingbird
whose wings
vibrate your name
from a jasmine flower.

You will learn drought,
the blood-cursed order
of things, soon enough.
Loaded down, a burro
plods into the storm.
Dark seed survives
where other plants do not.

Each morning rooster
and bell acclaim you.
Still, ancestral voices lie
trapped beneath the cobblestones.
If you braid your hair
you will go deaf,
so let it plunge from

your shoulders and free them.
Corn grows tall from its roots.
In these latitudes
innocence colors itself copper.
Hold it close,
and when you find a good man,
take him deep underwater.

The View from My Hotel Room at the Posada de las Monjas

It's a cell, this room,
an abode for an anchorite
tending ravens in his beard.
El Greco could have painted here,
St. Anthony prayed until his hands
betrayed his own stigmata,
a monk impaled his life

on a bed of nails.
But let's be charitable:
what do I love if not
these severe, simple lines
that suggest passion whelmed into wood,
austerity that burns like thighs
in the night mind where the cock crows loudest?

When light
streams through the open window
I lie back to receive it
dreaming of Sor Juana de la Cruz,
of salvation embraced
by the spectrum.
From my terrace

I savor the town of San Miguel.
No denial in these domes and cupolas,
the walls drenched with color:
carmine and pink,
seaside shades of blue.
And the stout woman who sweeps
the gutter clean,

blouse aflame
with the age-old secret of fire,
laughs as her broom evicts
the crumbling skull of Cortés.

Here it is all about *becoming*,
a filigree of smoke
rising through palm and bougainvillea

until neither earth
nor sky can contain it.

Light in San Miguel

Here where the empty mirror burns
clarity leaps, turns deftly surgical.
The hummingbird suspended above bougainvillea
raises its young on just such nectar,
knowing their metabolism requires it,
demands nothing impure.

What river, flowing back upon itself,
gives birth to copper?
Who rakes the talon on the wall?
Transfixed by the fusion
of sky and salmon-hued cathedral,
I scuff the gravel of past lives:

Maybe Vermeer, painting in the 1600s,
was Euclid centuries before,
prepared for color
by first mastering angle and line.
Blissed on mathematics, on form
as divinity itself,

a plangent bell within the garden.
Isn't it possible a medieval pilgrim
walking for months to Santiago de Compostela
had some inkling of this, shared
a similar goal, a beauty that stung?
That opened him like a scalpel,

bled from him a bilious humor
so he could begin to heal the fracture
of a mauve heart, reconcile square and circle,
vermilion and the cold, maddened eye?

I feel this now in the *Jardín*
after they've hosed the flagstones down.
That my trembling hand craves lavender.
That the rooster can predict what's coming.

A Nun's Tale
for Lois

Though neither Catholic nor Christian,
you enter this church in Guanajuato.
An old, half-remembered song has drawn
you here, a devotional candle whose pale
tongue flickers when you curl upon
yourself, a wave pouring over its crest.

You seem so natural on your knees,
a cloister child yearning for sisterhood.
That opaque mantle of silence
in which the rustle of a habit
across the cold stone floor crackles
with a kiss, a fleeting touch denied.

A routine quick to become familiar:
terce, vespers, matins,
bells tolling for a door pulled shut
as they herald canonical hours.
And all the while ecstasy mushrooms

like a fetus, a glorious weed
crowding out inferior plants.
A stalk you climb with intent:
the long, slow plunge
into a godhead of fire and roses.

But we are speaking of today, this life.
Bowed over interlocking hands,
you don't see the pigeon
just below the ceiling
flap its wings,
then plummet across the nave.

The stunning arc of its descent,
like a plane
curtailing its dive
at the last possible second,
propels it through a side door
into brilliant, windswept blue.

Short Men with Guns, Panajachel, Guatemala

The President knows everything.
    —Miguel Ángel Asturias, *El Señor Presidente*

The way metal barrels grow like branches
from their arms. Sketch the language of leaves.

Two guards, semi-automatics slung over their shoulders,
swing open the bank doors to let me in.

Their voices white foam, a flutter of silk.
And the teeth illuminating their dark brown faces

picket fences of denial.
So polite, as if the weapons themselves

were manicured, the bullets half-moons
revealed with the cuticle pared back.

Deferring to the gringo
with dollars to exchange for quetzales.

Not like *índios* wiped out in the war or herded
into *polos de desarollo,* the re-education camps.

Roberto, where are they taking you? Tomás,
the chickens! I am bleeding feathers...

The voices then slivers of ironwood. The manicures
seared like pork, a weather that leaked acid rain.

The smoke when the huts were burning:
Don't you miss it, Javier?

Earth Oracle: Llanganuco, Peruvian Andes

At Chinan Cocha, most seductive of lakes,
aquamarine reinvents the eye.
This is a color Vermeer would have

sealed in a vault, gone to his knees
before a witch to transmit from his brush.
Pure as wind, a falcon in flight,

its lavish sheen dazzles no sense
more than the mind itself. Such a shade,
querida, rends the veil of smoke each of us

weaves at a dusty loom. This world,
our own reflection, bears our indelible stamp.
What to make, then, of the Christ statue

built on the mudflow that buried Yungay?
Palms outstretched, burdened by impotence,
a futility bred into these mountains

for centuries that declares nothing, sister,
can be done. *Así es*, as the saying goes,
and when a dark rain begins to fall

embers will surely drown. Dare we
think of that salvation passed down
as simply a hired hand we've put to work

stringing fence wire, an outrider rounding up
our miseries to sell at auction? And if so,
what does that say to these hardy high

altitude shrubs? The condor's dipped wing?
Imagine Plato when he visualized Ideal Form.
Arising thunderstruck, out of his head

as he stumbled back to Athens half-blinded
by the weld of concept and color. Deliverance
a cirrus cloud, body a cipher ransacked below.

First Night, Ecuadorean Amazon

Indians, their voices
    a murmur of smoke,
        prepare for sleep.

Eco-tourists
    follow their lead.
        A heavy rain

spatters the broad
    leaves of banana trees
        in the clearing,

hisses in blackness
    like steam.
        Something within me

is dying so that something else,
    streaked with chlorophyll
        and water, may be born.

I rock in my hammock
    attended by jaguars
        who recite García Lorca.

All the jungle is a prayer.
    Only the monkeys shouting
        from the forest canopy

disregard this music:
    pelting one another
        with dung-smeared copies

of *Time* magazine,
    they argue all along
        the slick wet saddle of night.

Mayan Women Balancing Bundles on Their Heads, Guatemala

You would see them along the highland roads
or gracing Calle Santander in Panajachel,
movements like blue water, clouds you could gather up.

You thought of earth, of bark and honeycomb,
volcanic dreams suddenly seeded with ash.
How the dyes of their clothing beckoned

to the sluggish stream calcifying your bones.
How it quickened, then flooded the fields with silt.

Lima Hotel

My room, slightly larger than a closet, is on the roof.
Monkeys and parrots mingle with the skinned hides
of caimans and jaguar pelts above the bathroom door.

Ill, a long bus ride with vultures and vomit behind me,
I read Michener and lurch toward the toilet
whenever my body trembles. The tiny monkey

who rummages through the sugar bowl on my breakfast table
reminds me that this morning only he is God.

Monument

Have you seen the statue of Pizarro in Lima?
On a rearing horse, sword in hand, he commands.
What we don't see, of course, are Indians trampled

beneath the hooves. Nor has the sculptor carved
the myriad screams that even today haunt the air
like mist that never drops its moisture.

Cut off, they hang over the city's dirty yellow
buildings, laundry torn from a line.

Through the Looking Glass

What was I seeking two miles high in the Andes?
Not goose-stepping soldiers, but they were there.
Nor coconut vendors splitting the shells with machetes.

I'd read my *Lonely Planet* guide. I knew the gemstones
scattered through its pages. But one afternoon over tea,
when Maoist guerrillas were plotting death in Lima

and Ayacucho, Héctor Ponce de León raised this
question with his cup: *Have you read Henry Miller?*

Flor, a Peruvian Schoolgirl

I took her photo twenty years ago,
when guerrillas fueled like a prairie fire
terrorized their way toward a lost Inca past.

We met in the Huancayo market, her name
one of those apt and inexplicable strokes of fortune,
like a perfect circle by Giotto. Because it's true

she blossoms, unfolds her petals with that artless
faith one finds in pilgrims, a peony's rich blush.
.

What Gets Passed Down

I can tell him there's no Kansas in Peru,
no corn and wheat rolling to the horizon.
I can invoke schools, roads, infrastructure.

But what is Kansas compared to horse soldiers
armed with God? The sword of gold and slave labor?
He's seen me reading *Conquest of the Incas*,

and now he wants to know: *Why are you so rich
and we, with all our mineral resources, so poor?*

Martín

Violinist, mountaineer, he forced a guy in charge
of the music to play Mozart in a Peruvian bar.
Led me over a trail where one slip could kill.

Defeated by ice near the summit of Artesonraju,
he bitched and got drunk in Huaraz. Lanterns
cast the only light, the power station bombed out.

That night on a street corner, his Slovenian dirge
of farewell lifted even the stones from their beds.

Oriente

They were a virus with no known cure,
those jungle oil towns. Something that
corroded, gnawed like ravenous ants.

Mud, potholes, lakes of water in the street,
the half-naked locals a fungus
as they nursed their colas: torpor.

Until our canoe moved out on the river.
Until, like butterflies in shadow, we launched.

Photograph, Amazon Basin, Ecuador

A Sione Indian chief and his shaman wear blue
tunics and necklaces made of boars' teeth. Jeinaro
can put a dart through a banana at fifty paces. Charra

knows the secrets of the trumpet vine. Not that this
will count when the modern world abducts them.
This morning they paint symbols on our faces

with reverent care. After a hike through the jungle,
rain blurs, then wipes away their meaning.

Amazon Flashback

After dinner in a one-room structure made of ironwood
and palm thatch, Indians lean back and smoke.
Patricio, our guide, describes step by step

the process to shrink a head. I think of my father
among the Shuar in 1929, the freshly severed head
he photographed on the ground. How surprised

it would be if it could open its eyes tonight.
What it would make of heavy metal.

New Year's Day in San Miguel

From my hotel room I look down into gardens,
into courtyards of people living side by side.
At geraniums, hibiscus, poinsettias like blood stars.

At palms and a giant mimosa. The small
poodle humping its larger companion.
I'm thinking about the view into this room

when a rooster tells the whole damn neighborhood
about the guy wandering naked in number 53.

Question

He asked me how I liked his country. I thought
of the bus I had just ridden, floorboards so trashed
I could see the road underneath. I thought of the Army

patrolling the streets of Ayacucho, of guerrillas
and assassins, inflation over the moon, of the woman
in the Huancayo market who said gringos knew nothing.

I thought of the highland Indians, how the beautiful
sadness of their music clung to the valleys like mist.

Tracking The Minotaur

A Chance Encounter

Because she had once married a Greek
because I'd traveled to Greece in the '60s
because we were visiting a mutual friend
on the Upper West Side,
we had this conversation.
And though I protested when she sat down
that I had to get some sleep
she insisted on just one small glass of wine.
Which became two and then three
as we agreed that where Kazantzakis was transcendent,
Sartre was empty and Hemingway merely small.
Her hands spoke passion,
as if releasing flocks of doves into her voice,
a soft liqueur blend of European Texas
that drew me into that old yearning
for the expatriate life,
for garnet angels
and mandolins raining down on Russia
and I thought yes,
there's that chorus in the blood,
the one that's attended all our births:
to track the minotaur,
the iron tyranny of *things*,
to find it and destroy it with the dance,
with epiphanies of water,
swinging up onto its head
like a naked acrobat
as light pours in from the sea.

The Train to Athens
for John

Ever since Munich they've been with us,
stuffed into our compartment
smelling of the Mediterranean,
that pungent mix of garlic and sweat
that makes us feel the only life
worth living takes place
in funky markets
where the action never stops.

They're going home, these Greeks,
their flimsy cardboard luggage
filling the corridors
like junk in an abandoned attic.
They share their olives, bread, cheese, salami,
which we chase with Riesling wine.
All the way down
Yugoslavia's hot central valley
thirst rages like a brushfire,
our only option soda pop so bad
our stomachs take monastic vows.
No water, no sleep, Belgrade drab
but for Albanians in sheepskin caps.
In the war museum,
a mock fight with swords
and drawings of Turkish impalers.

At a Macedonian watering hole
women rush the train with melons,
their outstretched arms
straining to reach us as if
handing over babies
just ahead of advancing bayonets.

Would this happen in America?
They could have come
from one of those Marx Brothers movies
where gypsies dance simply because they're gypsies,
unaware they're even poor—
except these women know because their bones
accuse them every morning before dawn.

You nod, looking so Beat
in your beret and black turtleneck.
We long to follow them back to the village,
stay among pigs and corn for months.

The truth, when it reveals itself,
rises like fog from a distant plain:
These are the desperate ones,
the emigrants who wind up in Cleveland.

One last town before the Greek border.
Skopje smells of oil.

Epiphanal

Two men enter the café
and toss a bandana on the floor.
They begin to dance, as ordained
in Greece as whitewash and lamb.

The shorter one leaps and locks
his legs around his partner's waist.
Bends backward until it seems
he must break while the tall man,

snapping his fingers to the beat,
fashions a slow, measured weave.
With his teeth Shorty plucks the bandana
before his legs release their grip.

All the while, lamb and beer keep coming,
the sizzling meat flung toward us
on sheets of wax paper. We eat,
we drink, we kick star dreams

from the rocky road after villagers
drag us outside into their circle
Joy, I know, is transitory, a fickle guest,
a seed pod scattered, denied.

But when I relieve myself against a wall
it undulates in 5/8 time.
Here even the stones are oceans.
Tossed like a fishing smack

on heave and spray,
I negotiate the yawning depths
without compass, charts, wheel.
Become a trawler of the night.

Athena Parthenos

From this rubble,
    these shattered blocks
        strewn about the temple floor,

I look down upon the *agora*,
    the ancient marketplace.
        Across the whitewashed city

the port of Piraeus hugs the Aegean
    smelling of fish,
        its nets bulging with sponges.

I could go there, drawn by gangplanks
    and the buried image
        of a trireme.

But I've climbed this rock because
    they were *here*. Long before Christ,
        revering a goddess of wisdom.

Some have never left.
    Still cursing the plague
        that carried off Pericles

when Athens needed him most,
    they rehash "virtue" and "the good."
        Though I cannot see them,

they cling to fluted marble
    as tightly as to their past,
        wondering what went so wrong

that they would linger
　　ever since, wearing loss
　　　　like a garment stained with wine.

I want to tell them it is the way of things,
　　that crystal breaks and the jagged
　　　　cry sticks in the throat,

but they no longer hear. Even dust
　　baking on the stony pathway
　　　　robs them of their birthright.

It's enough to turn
　　a quarter moon upside down,
　　　　to make me ask

how many places we can call home.
　　If the small Indiana town
　　　　ringed by soybean fields

or the suburban house
　　four miles from the mall
　　　　are merely points of departure,

yolk sac for the greater journey,
　　what of the cry of the sandhill crane
　　　　along the Platte,

the copper vessel, thousands of years old,
　　on whose surface
　　　　your sister lies with a king?

Carve your name
　　on a shag bark hickory
　　　　and memory floods the roots.

These are my companions now,
   these wandering shades
      deprived of bodies,

polis, a shared incandescence.
   They know the fickle horse,
      the headstrong rider.

Jealous of limbs
   that bend and uncurl at will,
      they mimic fire from a bowl.

Barter the harsh braying of mules.

When Alan Bates Meets Irene Pappas on a Country Road in *Zorba*

Think first of heat,
radiation of white stones
spewed from the earth's core
to congeal on dry, sunburnt hills,

think of dust
like the breath of a consumptive
contaminating bush and rock,
silence an enervating shimmer,

think of time squeezed
like layered plates under a Mesozoic sea,
how it cracks, moans,
succumbs.

It is the world before the world
and she is of it, the widow,
black boots, black hair,
eyes of dark lava

from which accusations flow
as from armor rusting in ashheaps,
from marble pillars
where whole armies once made

smoky offerings to the gods.
This is the story told by her heel
as it strikes the path,
the poem inscribed on a blade of iron.

And the Englishman? He squints
through eyes stung with sweat,
filled with dread
because nothing has prepared him,

shy writer
whose mouth is full of pebbles,
for the sound of the drum
when his bones shatter into pure air.

We see it clearly from a distance:
the inevitable slowing down,
the words dropped stillborn from their tongues
as they draw parallel for an instant.

And when their eyes lock, do you hear
the baked stones turn upon themselves
in their agony, all the dead warriors
cry out from their graves at once?

Apollo in the Time of *John Wesley Harding*

Trying to hitch a ride in Greece back then
was like splitting open a sparrow's gut
to find omens in the road's harsh glare.
No way to change one's fortune.
Out here only the gods would provide.
More often than not they spurned me,

and that, too, was cloth spun by the Fates.
I came to know heat and dust and silence
better than I knew my friends,
better, even, than my own past.
I could depend on them,
and when they appeared, as they always did,
they punished me like a blowtorch.

But he was real, all right,
burly and hairy-armed, melons bouncing
in the truck bed as he throttled down.
When I climbed aboard hunger swung up behind me.
He nodded and found a café deep in the hills.
We ordered omelettes, sliced the melons.
Dropping a coin in the jukebox
he began to dance, snapping his fingers

like kindling, his movements alchemical,
a sweep of tidewater across the floor.
This is what brought me from another world:
someone who could flare like an orchid
simply because blood rose in Orion.
From the Bosporus
I'd been tempted by Bulgaria,
the mask of a hard-line Stalinist state,

but the gods decreed otherwise.
They'd had a plan all along.
Men don't do this in America. Not alone,
exposed, subject to free fall and shame.
It's too taxing, wearing chain mail,
to raise one's arms high enough
for the fledgling nesting there
    to lift off.

Orpheus

On a country road in Greece,
just after the coup that denied Papandreou,
we met an army column on a break.
You could hitch for hours
in that dusty heat and never see a car.
The sun blazed down with the full
weight of Classical history,
that burden
of the fountainhead of Western Civilization,
the air smelling like herbs
as it must have in Plato's day,
and while, unknown to us,
in the name of anti-Communism the Colonels
were cranking up the torture machine
through which rags soaked in urine and excrement
were forced down terrified throats,
vaginas ripped, tubes conducting water
at extreme pressure
rammed up the quivering anus,
a young soldier who earned
a fraction per month
of what we traveled on per week
reached into his knapsack,
pulled out a dark brown loaf
of bread and handed it over,
like Socrates refusing any thought
of payment for this, his own philosopher's stone.

The Way It Was

Isn't the first time a thorn
draws blood the one we honor?

In Athens I entered light that defied
the body, made me a dandelion
anointed by wind.
I've seen the same in Santa Fe,
color so sharp it bled the sky,
so pure it told my fortune.

Each morning I drank juices mixed with pulp.
Poured them down so the moon would ride
a bull's horns and the hot stones crow their thirst.
I could taste the poor, gritty soil when I swallowed,
feel the rough hands that trimmed and grafted trees
so their fruit would swell like breasts.

Bouzouki players in outdoor *tavernas*
showered notes like silver dollars,
beads of spray that held my own reflection.
I needed that then, needed rhythm
and time signatures crooked as a stick,
docks and waves and sponges

hauled up from a blue that blessed.
All that the land could give me,
each herbal breath. Even the donkey
plodding up a sun-baked slope.

Something the dark bird had stolen.
Piece by piece returned.

Inside the Blue Mosque, Istanbul

Say the word aloud, say *blue,*
and the mind teems with guests:
Renoir, Vermeer, Gainsborough's *Blue Boy,*
Picasso's Blue Period, the lines
from a Mark Doty crab poem:
a shocking Giotto blue.

Say *blue,* and a marlin taildances on the water,
a slide guitar spells heartache in plural.
Woke up this mornin', I believe I'll dust my broom.
Frida lives on in *la Casa Azul.*
And the beggar trapped in a hash dream haze
hails bands of blue men from the Sahara.

Say *blue,* and doors swing wide open.
To speak it here adds yet another
tile to the thousands already present.
Did Gershwin divine such a rhapsody?
Such a dazzling faience mosaic?
Or is blue encoded in our cells,

a script for the primal color of being?
Look around. When you left your shoes
at the door, didn't you slough off
your skin so blue could breathe,
could curl phantom-like among the pillars,

a counterpoint
to the slow, steady rhythm
of a cobbler tapping out his blood
beat in the bazaar, circa 1650?
Blue. It haunts the back alleys,

a companion for the road, for the long haul,
for daughter and courtesan a final recumbent address.
First water, last silence, the country in between.
Blue Danube. Blue bayou. *Cordon bleu.*
The heron and the kingfisher. Blue.

Pogrom

Came on a cloudless day
when the heat bore down
came as surf
a dark speck vomited on the horizon
came scything and threshing from the Don

      the swollen Dnieper

came drenched on a Cossack saber
came where coins were half counted
and yeast refused to rise
came for the daughter
the strong seed in her belly

came for the fire immune to water
for the grain and the cloth
and the long shank of terror
came for menorah and timbrel
the vestments abandoned in flight

came for the lamb and the jewel-eyed cock
came for the Law
for the Book and the tablets
came above all for the color
the red streak staining the village

came to harvest
scatter
plow under

came as wind to erase
stamp out

reeking of smoke
of sweat and rank leather

came riding
came screaming

came

Dry Rain at Terezin

Looking at the narrow wooden coffins
the camp inmates built, you wonder
how they squeezed even malnourished bodies

into them before the crematory took over.
Wedged like pitons banged into the crevice
of a rock face. Almonds in their shells.

The wind screams in commentary,
bends poplars as if they were bows
launching invisible arrows of grief.

And leaves propelled like locusts
to the east flail the sky,
their anchor line to earth ripped out.

Chagall would understand this.
And the dead who seem without number.
Always circling. Trying to find a job.

Terezin Concentration Camp, Bohemia

Near the railway spur
bones still cry for water.

And the ashes?
Who can say what roots they nourish,
what borders they have crossed?

Here the ship never sails,
the shawl cannot cover.

Tell me silence isn't the loudest voice.

When the open mouth forgets itself,
the straw man drinks his shadow.

And the moon?
Gracing a wanted poster,

an impossible price on its head.

Coal-faced, it shuns the cattle cars
rolling east on tracks of tallow.

Absence. Isn't that the surest
footprint of a crime?
The song the mockingbird teaches its young?

This rain grazes the skin like rust.

Terezin Concentration Camp:
The Children's Drawings Speak

We are the witnesses
the true survivors
the tongues
still rooted to their source.

We streaks of orange crayon
stick figures and umbrella tree
birds pecking a hole in the sky.

We know the stars that fall
from the barrel of a gun,

the stench of terror
in the barracks.

But we do not record them.
Because they did not:

they who created us,
who drew a world

where a piano banished boots,
ignored the trains

that carried them
to the ash fields of Poland.

Within our borders

Jericho needed no walls
and Joshua's trumpet

gathered dust above the grain crib.
Fetch the fatted calf,

the ram caught by his horns
in a thicket.

What do museums and memorials do
if not keep us pinned to an event?

But these, they were thistles,
grass seed

scattered over salted ground.

Blades and shoots that poked through,
found their crooked way.

Return to the Kavárna Medúza

I imagine Kafka here. And Rilke:
flame informing a monk's cowl.
The kind that purifies, licks
away all excess, so that the body

takes on the luster of a scarab,
becomes transparent skin
stretched tight, pegged down,
a shelter with fire shining through.

In medieval times the Church
was sanctuary, first and last
recourse. Now we have
a cabin on a raging creek,

the deer startled by a pine cone.
Or this coffeehouse with an old piano
in the corner, a girl whose hips
are rivers flooding their banks.

June 4, 1989: Tienanmen

The moon hangs in the gibbets,
twisting on brittle threads of silk.
Across the square the daughter
of Wu Shu the tailor sits attended
by a hundred snowy geese
and furiously writes poems in blood.
As fast as she completes them
she flings them at advancing tanks.
A crane floats above the Yang-tze,
white banners tumbling from its beak.
All over the city graves are opening up
and releasing their dead masters.
Mao is the smoke that rolls
Jao-ling to her knees,
the furnace into which the Army
shovels the rubble of broken youth.
He rises above the pavement,
mouth set firmly in place
by fat worms
that never satisfy their hunger.
They crawl from his eyes
bloated in mantles of darkness
while soldiers bayonet the moon,
spilling three virgins practicing t'ai chi.
Instantly street dogs leap forward,
paws drumming the cobblestones
like silver hammers.

Where is Li Pei,
whose almond heart opened in a shower of petals
before the triumph of the hard men?

Water Suite
for Aung San Suu Kyi

It is the season of the monsoon in Burma.
As it has been since the junta seized power.
A rain that cancels, slashes like a bayonet.
Bleeds all it strikes.

Monks in saffron robes stream past your window.
You weep and pray,
know some will become red flowers
when spiders come out to bite.

Years under house arrest
have made you a copper lamp,
the nonperson no one forgets.
Danger can be a cobra or tropical disease,

and poor balance on the Irrawaddy
means a corpse flushed south of Rangoon.
But to the generals you are the fuse
that ignites the magazine,

more explosive than all their bombs.
Nothing so fatal as a mind that speaks itself.
Are reports leaking out mere rumors?
Thousands jailed, prisoners, it is whispered,

burned alive? Water doesn't care.
The road to Mandalay steams with loss.
Look in vain to Kipling's Rangoon pagoda
for the Buddha who gazed in silent non-attachment.

Where smoke from incensed joss sticks spirals
its delicate threads,
Gautama has abandoned his perch.
Taken to the streets with the crone

who begged at the gate.
Eyes outlined with turmeric dust,
she grimaces through worn teeth blackened
by betel nut. Shakes a feeble fist.

Lotus Eaters, Katmandu
for Hansdieter

You wrote about the tinned cupboard full of hash
at the government store, the ganja brigades you passed
on your way to the Blue Tibetan. The pain

of leaving Buddha robes and cruel-faced gods behind
when you rode a truck south to India. How images
of dreamy eyes, of Chinese Baba counting his money

while the smoke-hazed gypsy woman graced
your bed flaked from you like dried blood.

Tagong: the Wild West

A pack of dogs roams the muddy street
that bisects this one-horse Tibetan town,
and a dead one stains the sidewalk with its corpse.

Rough-looking Khampas gather by their motorbikes.
In the clinic, a young Chinese doctor
gives me a three-hour IV and a shot to bring

my fever down. *Obama*! he says. *Kobe*!
On the mountainside, prayer flags thick as stars.

Tagong Temple

Walking past the smell of raw sewage,
I continue up a muddy track to the first row
of prayer wheels. Others have hurried

on ahead. At each great drum cylinder
I grasp the wooden handle and push it
forward, my conversation with you, my father,

flowing from my arm. Who knew the body could
speak such syllables? Such pure, eloquent language?

Early Morning in Tibet

Still dark when I leave Tagong, its red-
robed monks. Two days before, the man
dashing down an alley, horse in tow, as water

poured from the sky. And the Chinese? Wayward
smoke. Weapons dormant, yet ready to bloom
like nightshade. Yaks in our headlights wander

across the road. Pulling over, my driver scatters
prayers scrawled on post-it notes to the wind.

Sky Burial

Mao, you grubby bastard, your face peers out
from a 50-yuan note, almost benign, the famous wart
fixed to the fleshy chin. And on the opposite side,

the Potola Palace in Lhasa. With your blessing, 6,000
monasteries destroyed, Norbu sentenced to fifteen years for
raising a Tibetan flag. Lhasa throbs with propaganda

and men in riot gear. Only vultures crowding a hacked corpse
know the Long March dissolves in the heart of the lotus.

Teahouse: Chengdu, China

Not a tea*house*, exactly, but a glorified hole in the wall
down a side street from Wenshu Monastery. The awning
derelict, half collapsed with branches and leaves.

The same men every afternoon gambling at cards
in the heat, and couples who play *mah-jongg*.
An old man pours for me, I pour for him.

The glass sears my palm.
Next time I won't have to pay.

Two Charcoal Drawings from Central Asia

One Uzbek, the other Tajik. These turbaned tribesmen
bookend the bow hung on my bedroom wall.
Artifacts from my father's life in jungle and steppe.

I cannot see their hands, but I know their gnarled,
rough beauty, so like the wayward contours of oak.
And weathered faces resigned to a moon's coy tricks.

Invisible between them, my father rides eastward.
This morning the world comes on the wind.

Tangier in the Age of Aquarius

What did we know? We were young, which meant
innocence coined and redeemed like gold.
Each day brought hustlers, incense, mint tea

so rich it purged us of all our petty crimes.
Granted unlimited license. And when the sun
went down over the medina it took us with it,

trolled us like moonlight through alleys
where we molted, then renewed our skins.

Old Men Who Sleep on the Ground, Marrakech Market

Curled up in *djellabas* by their stalls, they begin
to stir. When they rise, beards hang
from faces that have known

the night of a thousand camels. Slowly
they come alive behind mounds of nuts
and fruit and battered scales of brass.

With each glass of mint tea you feel compelled
to worship light, the glory of their hands.

The Mother of All Markets

Monsieurs, a boy asks, *you are leaving Marrakech?*
Brian and I are walking out of the Djemaa el Fna,
the beyond crazy heart of the medina, the moon

a silver dirham above the crenellated Koutoubia Mosque.
Yes, we say, recalling three blind beggars,
the dancers, drummers, tribesmen, women in veils.

Yes, we are leaving. Leaving Marrakech.
And oh the regret, my son, the regret!

The Murder of Lorca

Because his words were cadenzas of dark waters
they came for him: men of pus and waxed paper,
men who gnawed their own tongues. Who lives

in the bell tower? Tells one's fortune with metal?
Release a falcon, pull the hood from his eyes,
and rain begins to fall. Blood on the moon

means black earth, the prodigal mending
his sandals. The brass oil lamp. Flickering.

What I Saw in Seville

What *wasn't* there. Walking those whitewashed
neighborhoods I felt the Moor at my shoulder.
Fountains gushed into Arabic courtyards. Wrought

iron grillwork adorned the balconies. Men without women,
without even guitars, clapped their hands together
and danced to the staccato beat of their blood.

Here bullion poured in from the New World.
Here Columbus took ship, sword pointed west.

Author Note

Peter Ludwin, *b. 1942*, has been active in the arts as a poet and folk musician. For the past eleven years he has been a participant in The San Miguel Poetry Week in de Allende, Mexico. In 2007, Ludwin received a Literary Fellowship from Artist Trust. He was the 2007-2008 Second Prize Winner of the Anna Davidson Rosenberg Awards, a finalist for both the 2010 and 2011 Gival Press Poetry Award and received Special Merit Recognition in the 2011 Muriel Craft Bailey Memorial Award Competition. He is a 2009 and 2010 Pushcart Prize nominee. Ludwin has been a featured reader for the Distinguished Writers Series (Tacoma, WA), the John R. Milton Writer's Conference (Vermillion, SD) and at Whittier College (Los Angeles, CA). He has studied under noted poets such as Mark Doty, Tony Hoagland and C.K. Williams. Ludwin's poetry has appeared in many journals, among them *Antietam Review, California Quarterly, The Comstock Review, Hawai'i Pacific Review, Midwest Quarterly, Nimrod, North American Review, Prairie Schooner, Quercus Review, South Carolina Review, South Dakota Review* and *Whiskey Island Magazine.* His poetry is influenced by American folk music, the natural world and the dynamics between Old World/New World perceptions.

Contemporary Poetry Titles Available From Presa Press

John Amen
  At the Threshold of Alchemy. ISBN: 978-0-9800081-5-9; 86 pgs.; $13.95.
Guy R. Beining
  nozzle 1-36. Chapbook; 44 pgs.; $6.00.
Louis E. Bourgeois
  Alice. Chapbook; 40 pgs.; $6.00.
Kirby Congdon
  Selected Poems & Prose Poems. ISBN: 978-0-9772524-0-4; 84 pgs.; $15.00.
  Athletes. ISBN: 978-0-9831251-0-5; 52 pgs.; pp; $9.95.
Hugh Fox
  Blood Cocoon - Selected Poems of Connie Fox. ISBN: 978-0-9740868-9-7; 72 pgs.; $15.00.
  Time & Other Poems. Chapbook; 44 pgs.; $6.00.
  Beyond Our Control - Two Collaborative Poems (with Eric Greinke). Special Edition Chapbook; 28 pgs.; $10.00.
Eric Greinke
  Selected Poems 1972-2005. ISBN: 978-0-9740868-7-3; 140 pgs.; $20.00
  Wild Strawberries. ISBN: 978-0-9800081-1-1; 96 pgs.; $15.00.
  Traveling Music. ISBN: 978-0-9800081-9-7; 84 pgs.; $11.95.
Kerry Shawn Keys
  The Burning Mirror. ISBN: 978-0-9772524-9-7; 92 pgs.; $14.95.
  Book Of Beasts. ISBN: 978-0-9800081-4-2; 64 pgs.; $12.95.
  Transporting, A Cloak of Rhapsodies. ISBN: 978-0-9800081-8-0; 112 pgs.; $15.95.
  Night Flight. ISBN: 978-0-9831251-3-6; 96 pgs.; $15.95.
Arthur Winfield Knight
  High Country. Chapbook; 40 pgs.; $6.00.
  Champagne Dawns. Chapbook; 28 pgs.; $6.00.
Richard Kostelanetz
  PO/EMS. Chapbook; 40 pgs.; $6.00.
  More Fulcra Poems. Chapbook; 36 pgs.; $6.00.
  Purling Sonnets. Chapbook; 32 pgs.; $6.00.
Ronnie M. Lane
  Morpheus Rising. Chapbook; 40 pgs.; $6.00.
Linda Lerner
  Living In Dangerous Times. Chapbook; 52 pgs.; $6.00.
Donald Lev
  Only Wings - 20 Poems of Devotion. Chapbook; 28 pgs.; $6.00.
Lyn Lifshin
  In Mirrors. ISBN: 978-0-9772524-3-5; 84 pgs.; $15.00.
  Lost Horses. Chapbook; 48 pgs.; $6.00.
Gerald Locklin
  From a Male Perspective. Chapbook; 32 pgs.; $6.00.

Glenna Luschei
Seedpods. Chapbook; 40 pgs.; $6.00.
Total Immersion. ISBN: 978-0-9800081-0-4; 96 pgs.; $15.00.
Witch Dance. ISBN: 978-0-9800081-7-3; 84 pgs.; $13.95.
Leaving It All Behind. ISBN: 978-0-9831251-2-9; 104 pgs.; $15.95.
Sprouts. Chapbook; 28 pgs.; $6.00.
Stanley Nelson
Pre-Socratic Points & Other New Poems. ISBN: 978-0-9772524-4-2; 84 pgs.; $15.00.
Limbos For Amplified Harpsichord. ISBN: 978-0-9772524 -8-0; 144 pgs.; $17.95.
City Of The Sun. ISBN: 978-0-9800081-2-8; 126 pgs.; $15.95.
Roseanne Ritzema, (Editor)
Inside The Outside - An Anthology of Avant-Garde American Poets.
ISBN: 978-0-9772524-1-1; 304 pgs.; $29.95.
Lynne Savitt
The Deployment Of Love In Pineapple Twilight. Chapbook; 48 pgs.; $6.00.
Steven Sher
Grazing On Stars - Selected Poems. ISBN: 978-0-9831251-7-4; 84 pgs.; $15.95.
Harry Smith
Little Things. ISBN: 978-0-9800081-3-5; 78 pgs.; $13.95.
t. kilgore splake
ghost dancer's dreams. ISBN: 978-0-9831251-4-3; 68 pgs.; $12.95.
coming home. Chapbook; 36 pgs.; $6.00.
Lloyd Van Brunt
Delirium. Chapbook; 48 pgs.; $6.00.
Marine Robert Warden
Beyond The Straits. ISBN: 978-0-980001-6-6; 72 pgs.; $13.95.
A.D. Winans
This Land Is Not My Land. Chapbook; 48 pgs.; $6.00.
The Other Side of Broadway - Selected Poems. ISBN: 978-0-9772524-5-9; 132 pgs.; $18.00.

Exclusive European distribution through
Gazelle Book Service Ltd.
White Cross Mills, Hightown,
Lancaster, LA1 4XS, UK
sales@gazellebooks.co.uk   www.gazellebooks.co.uk

Available through Baker & Taylor, The Book House,
Coutts Information Services, Midwest Library Services,
local bookstores & directly from the publisher -www.presapress.com